CORPS VALUES

ZELL MILLER

LONGSTREET PRESS
ATLANTA, GA

Published by LONGSTREET PRESS, INC.,
a subsidiary of Cox Newspapers,
a subsidiary of Cox Enterprises, Inc.
2140 Newmarket Parkway
Suite 122
Marietta, Georgia 30067

Printed in the United States of America

1st printing, 1997

Library of Congress Catalog Number 96-79800

ISBN: 1-56352-387-6

Jacket design by Jill Dible
Book design and typesetting by Neil Hollingsworth

We must remember that one man is much the same as another, and that he is best who is trained in the severest school.

Thucydides,
Great Peloponnesian War (431-404 B.C.)

PROLOGUE

Drunk.

Dirty, disheveled and dejected, I sat crosslegged on the floor of the Gilmer County Jail in the Appalachian town of Ellijay, Georgia. It was a hot Saturday night in August of 1953.

Drunk out of my skull from rot-gut moonshine liquor, I had side-swiped a car and run headlong into a ditch. Within minutes I was handcuffed, thrown into the back of the sheriff's car and carted off to where I belonged.

Behind bars with me were four others, all of us in the same dark cell. Three old, grizzled mountaineers in bib overalls and a "dandy" in seersucker pants and what had once been a white starched shirt. And me. All were older and all were just as drunk as I was.

I was 21 years old. One thing was clear in my woozy head: I was in a bad, bad situation and it was no one's fault but my own.

Certainly not my mama's. Birdie Bryan Miller had raised me and my sister alone, a "single mother" long before that term became well known. My father had died when I was 17 days old. My mama didn't just do the best she could; she did the best anyone could. She raised us in a loving home, took us to church twice each Sunday, taught us about values and read to us. *The Little Engine That Could* was my favorite story.

We grew up in a house built from rocks that my mother had hauled out of a nearby creek. My six-year-old sister watched me on a blanket under a tree near the creek while my mother stooped and lifted and waded in that cold mountain water day after day as she stacked hundreds of beautiful, smooth rocks on the creek bank.

Today, that rock house is the Miller home place and, in certain places, her handprints in the concrete are still visible.

Her handprints were on me as well. And that night I sat in jail with my head in my hands wondering how anyone could have sunk so low. How could anyone have done their mother so wrong?

The life into which I was born in the mountain environment of all-white Towns County, Georgia, in 1932 was as different as night is from day from the metropolitan, multicultural Atlanta, Georgia, I now live in. Poverty was as general then as it is stratified along class lines now. There were no race or religion problems, because we were all of the same color and similar Protestant persuasions. There were some family feuds and political rifts between Democrats and Republicans, but nothing even closely approximating the divisions and conflicts of modern, urban society.

However narrow or insular the outlook of the average citizen of my native area might have been, character — as personified by honesty and respect for parents, elders, peers and self — was taught by word and example and emulated by deed. Discipline was expected and, if necessary, enforced by hickory sticks and woodshed visits. Children had chores which they were expected to perform as faithfully and thoroughly as their school homework, and the youngster who "got a whippin'" at school could expect to get another when he or she got home. Teachers were regarded as sacrosanct as parents were.

Life was a serious business, and it was treated as such. Children were trained from the earliest to speak only when spoken to and to respond to their elders with the appropriate "Yes, sir" or "No, ma'am." Whining and "talking back," or "sassin'," were certain to bring swift retribution.

My mother was a talented artist who was regarded by some as an independent and free spirit and different in her ideas and approach to life's trials and tribulations. But she worked twice as hard as any man I ever knew to educate her two children. My maiden aunt, Verdie Miller, was a teacher of awesome presence, a demanding taskmaster, and loving confidant. I also had an English teacher, Edna Herren, who was a major influence on me as a student.

But with all that I had going for me, I did not have a male role model in my life. And when I left my cocoon of insulated, mountain, female-dominated life, I found myself overly challenged and shockingly frustrated. The worldly, metropolitan atmosphere of Emory University in Atlanta was very different from the safe and sedate atmosphere of Young Harris College.

I felt overwhelmed by the sophistication of my fellow students, and for the first time — but not the last — had someone laugh at the twang of my "hillbilly" accent. The classes were harder, the students more articulate, and I became lonely, miserable, and depressed. A feeling of inferiority permeated my whole being. Unlike the "Little Engine," I quit, dropped out, and returned to my mountain home, to the great disappointment of my mother, my aunt, and the arched brows of the town and college gentry, who had wondered if the orphaned boy would be able to make it in the real world. I began to drink, run wild, and finally wound up in that drunk tank in Ellijay.

And so when my buddy Max Nicholson finally came and bailed me out Sunday afternoon, I went home, cleaned up, and then, with my tail between my legs, sneaked onto the back pew of Sharp Memorial Methodist Church. As Pastor Tom Smith spoke at that Sunday evening service and the choir sang those old familiar hymns I knew by heart, I sat alone, surrounded by my shame.

I realized I needed more than the tender mercies of my little local church, more even than a strong mother and loving friends had been able to provide. I was heading in the wrong direction, and I knew it. My thoughts drifted back to a sign I had seen in Atlanta: "The Marines: We make men," it proclaimed. Then and there I decided either to cure or kill myself by signing up for a three-year enlistment in that elite outfit.

The kill almost came before the cure, but it was the turning point of my life. Everything that has happened to me since has been at least an indirect product of that decision, and, in the 12 weeks of hell and transformation that were Marine Corps boot camp, I learned the values of achieving a successful life that have guided and sustained me on the course which, although sometimes checkered and detoured, I have followed ever since. That weak, mixed-up lad on the back pew never came back home; a strong, disciplined man in olive drab did. And when that guy quit at Emory, it was the last time he quit at anything.

The best analogy I have heard describing what it is like to go through Marine Corps boot camp is that it is the closest thing to a birth experience grown men will ever go through. The main difference is the gestation period is compressed into three instead of nine months.

Even the geography of Parris Island, South Carolina, site of Marine Corps boot camp, can be seen by a raw recruit as the equivalent of the female birthing anatomy. It is configured like a giant womb into which the only entry and exit is a two-mile-long causeway ending in a two-lane bridge over Archer's Creek, a tidal arm of Broad River. The base, which is surrounded by alligator-infested swamps, is the uterus, and the recruits, who are introduced into it in platoon-sized increments of approximately 74, are the fertilized eggs. The 65 or so who manage to take root and survive the rigorous and demanding training of the following 12 weeks subsequently emerge from the same channel as newborn Marines who will never again look upon life and its challenges as they did some 90 days earlier.

In the course of one season of the calendar, boot camp turns sometimes aimless youths into proud and self-disciplined Marines who have well-honed senses of self-esteem and dedication to themselves, their mission, and their country. The differences of economic classes and prejudices of race and religion which they brought with them have been transformed into respect for others and an ability to follow orders to achieve mutual goals.

Humorist Art Buchwald, one of the most famous alumni of the Marines, characterized his Corps training and discipline as "the right service in the right place at the right time." He called the experience "a very painful one, which is exactly how the Marines intend it to be," explaining that the purpose of boot camp is "to break you down, and then rebuild you into the person . . . who will never question an order, who will always worry about his buddy, and who, someday, will walk as tall as John Wayne."

That is also the goal of this book.

Of course, a lot of books have been written about values in the past few years. William Bennett had a best-seller, *The Book of Virtues*, and has made an industry out of speaking and writing about them from his point of view. I loved his book and bought copies for my children and, when his children's edition came out, gave copies to my grandchildren. I found myself in general — and, on some points, enthusiastic — agreement with most of his premises.

Even earlier, Robert Fulghum had a mega-literary hit with his *All I Really Need to Know I Learned in Kindergarten*. I devoured it, too, although it is obvious that I myself was a later bloomer in the achievement of such wisdom.

More recently, the entire nation was deluged during the 1996 Presidential campaign with debates and oratory about the national need for a renewal of "family values." This debate was highlighted by some rather pointed, and some-times personal, exchanges on what those values should be and how best to inculcate them in our children as guiding principles for successful lives. Whether it takes a "family" or a "village" — or, as I strongly believe, *both* — I do know that values young people learn as part of the growing-up process must be defined, refined, and etched into their per-sonalities and characters.

Values is a broad, generic term that has different mean-ings to different people. The fundamentalist Christian would have a different definition from that of the liberal-thinking philosopher, but I believe that on the basic, bedrock traits that constitute the foundation upon which successful lives are built there would be general agreement. And that is what this book is about — the insights I gained from experiencing and surviving the mind-expanding and soul-challenging ordeal of Marine Corps boot camp. I call them "Corps values."

Not everyone can join the Marines, and, quite frankly, the Marine Corps is not for everyone. But the basic lessons Marines teach their recruits are important ones. I believe that more of our citizens must learn these lessons if a democratic society in our republican form of government is to survive and thrive. I not only believe that with all my heart, but I also know it to be true from the lessons of my own life. I am as certain as the words on this page that I would not be in the position to write this book today had I not sought to "make a man of myself" by joining the Marine Corps as a troubled and insecure lad.

Like Art Buchwald, I remember my trips onto and out of Parris Island as if they were yesterday. I recall with clarity the thoughts I had about what I learned and what I must do to make those values a positive force in my life thereafter, regardless of what course it might take.

I made a list of those values on a piece of paper and have kept it in my pocket, and over the years, I have added to it. Also, over the years, the more I have thought about them, the more convinced I have become that these values constitute a formula for the survival of a society in which individuals can achieve for themselves and, at the same time, contribute to the advancement of mankind as a whole.

What are those values? I will list them now and then devote a brief chapter to each:

1. Neatness
2. Punctuality
3. Brotherhood
4. Persistence
5. Pride

6. Respect
7. Shame
8. Responsibility
9. Achievement
10. Courage
11. Discipline
12. Loyalty

Those who deride such qualities as generic generalizations simply have not thought them through.

Those who would contend that such attributes cannot be taught to individuals or groups without infringing upon their rights and beliefs simply miss the point that there are certain fundamental principles that underlie specific individual tenets of faith and belief. For example, one can have pride without being a racist, and one can practice brotherhood without forsaking or compromising adherence to one's religious or moral convictions.

I believe these are values that should be common to all people regardless of the color of their skin, the tenets of their denomination, or the places of their residence. I submit it is the only basis upon which diversity can coexist with commonality and all people can pursue individual goals for themselves while contributing to the general well-being and advancement of society as a whole.

Those who think otherwise need to go through twelve weeks of boot camp and see how they feel about it afterwards.

NEATNESS

"Neat" is a much-used word in the lexicon of contemporary youth, but its meaning and varying nuances have little relation to the not-so-subtle definition branded upon every aspect of the lives, conscious thoughts, and unconscious motivations of every recruit by the Marine Corps.

To many youth of today, being "neat" and doing "neat" things means either doing whatever everyone else is doing or doing whatever any individual wants to do regardless of the consequences to self or society. It is the total antithesis of what is "neat" as taught by the Marines, which is that the "only way to do everything is the right way, and the right way — without exception — is the Marine way."

I am old enough to remember the times in school when the teacher would make assignments or give examinations for which the instructions ended "and neatness will count." And the first lesson I learned as a Marine on my first days in boot camp at Parris Island was that neatness in everything not only is the norm in the Corps but also is the absolute minimum that will be tolerated. It is the standard by which every aspect of Marine life and performance is judged as satisfactory and acceptable.

My mother had always tried to instill in me that "cleanliness is next to godliness," but I quickly learned that the Marines insisted upon taking that concept one step higher by making it painfully clear that "neatness *is* godliness."

The Marine Corps believes that sloppiness is a sign of laziness while neatness is a sign of order and discipline, and, reduced to the individual level, a sloppy person is a dirty person while a neat person is a clean person. The Drill Instructors have a word for dirty recruits, "cruds," and "cruds" are not tolerated. When a recruit hears that dreaded word applied to him, any part of his gear, or any particular aspect of his performance, he knows he is about to get the "shape-up-or-ship-out" ultimatum.

The "neat" life for the Marine recruit begins with the "neat" Marine haircut and shower or scrubbing. The former takes less than 20 seconds and bloody woe to the recruit who fails to heed the admonition to put a finger on any mole or scalp blemish, because otherwise the barbers' clippers remove them with the hair which quickly piles up ankle deep at the base of each chair.

Next came shots for every disease under the sun, and then we were herded through showers like sheep on their way to slaughter. Our first issue of clothing was thrown at us and two pairs of brogans, or "boondockers," were draped around our necks. With caps yanked tightly down over our eyes and overloaded, new "sea bags" over our shoulders, we stumbled into ragged formation. That marked the beginning of twelve weeks of shouting, slapping, shoving, and kicking from the DIs (Drill Instructors) who vowed to teach us the meaning of neatness or, to use their term, being "squared away." That phrase had both physical and mental meanings: "neat and sharp" in the first instance and "having it together" in the second.

We learned quickly that the Corps does not tolerate trousers without creases, shoes that are not shined, ties that are too long or with a knot that isn't neat, belts that are too long, brass that is not shined, hair that is not closely clipped, side burns, or body odor. Tattoos were all right if they were about the Corps, the nation, or our mothers, and mustaches were okay after boot camp if they were neat. Caps have to be blocked just right, and a garrison cap may be only the width of two fingers above the eyes.

To this day it makes my Marine "blood" boil to see young people wearing caps and hats backward or, even worse, sideways. To my mind this is a symbol of lack of respect, and I suspect that most former Marines share my opinion.

My point is that good habits of personal grooming and dress learned in the Marine Corps will prevail for a lifetime.

Learning how to shave correctly was my first lesson in "neatness" on my second day as a recruit. Seventy-four of us were awakened at 0300 by a DI beating on a trash can, then we were herded into the "head" in our "skivvies," as our underwear shorts were called, to watch a DI shave the recruit he had chosen as the guinea pig of the day. Bleary eyes opened wide as we listened spellbound to a loud lecture which went like this:

"Now *that*, you idiots, is how you shave the Marine Corps way. You will shave the Marine Corps way every day. Do you understand?"

I have had that scene replayed before my morning mirror every day for more than four decades as I shave myself the Marine Corps way.

The shaving lesson quickly escalated into learning how to keep our "skivvies" clean. That instruction came with the announcement that we were going to be taught the correct "Marine Corps way to wipe your ass."

I can still repeat this little lecture verbatim, too.

"Some of you Cruds are going to wipe just half-assed, so I do not want to see any — and I mean *any* — dingleberries in your skivvies. You're going to have to drop your drawers from time to time, and I better not see one dingleberry in the ass of 'em."

One could almost hear 74 sphincters snapping to attention as we sang out "Yes, sir" while dire visions of "dingleberries" in our underwear danced in our heads.

That was a prelude to learning how to do laundry the Marine Corps way.

We were marched to a warehouse for what is known as "a bucket issue." Each of us received a galvanized gallon bucket, a large bar of lye soap, a scrub brush, and a bunch of one dozen (no more and no less) "tie-ties." These eight-inch lengths of heavy string, we were quickly to learn, were to be both our clothespins for hanging out laundry and the Corps' diabolical system for teaching us to keep track of and take care of all the equipment, clothing, and other items issued to us. A recruit could be called upon to account for his 12 "tie-ties" at any time, and heaven help anyone who could not come up with all of them under any and all circumstances; and the punishment for stealing another Marine's "tie-tie" was to be forced to run through a belt line — a row of fellow Marines authorized to whip your rear end.

Then the DI showed us the Marine Corps way to do our laundry, which is where the soap and brush came in. We used waist-high, concrete wash racks where we first lay all our clothes flat and stretched out. Then we wet and soaped them thoroughly. Next they were scrubbed completely on both sides with the brush and then thoroughly rinsed. Then they were hung on the clothes line using tie-ties in square knots. No one was allowed to deviate — even slightly — from this method.

Next followed equally meticulous instruction in making up one's "rack," as the bed is called. The DI and his assistants would force recruits to make their "racks" over and over until there was a perfect hospital fold at the bottom and the top was turned back with exactly twelve inches of sheet showing with a precise fold of six inches. We quickly learned to use our six-inch scrub brushes and our twelve-inch bayonets as rulers.

We were drilled in wearing our gear the exactly right,

"neat," Marine Corps way with everything from canteen straps to shoe laces always crossed left over right. We learned how to iron shirts with three sharp creases down the back and two sharp creases down the front through the middle of the pockets and to keep razor-sharp creases in our trousers by putting them on while standing on our lockers, never wearing them to sit on a commode, and getting our bunkmates to tie our shoes so we would not have to bend. We mastered the technique of spit shining our dress shoes by using only the index finger to apply Kiwi shoe polish and cold water with a clean scrap of a T-shirt and a slow, circular motion. (I still shine my own boots using the same proven technique.)

We further practiced folding our clothing and packing our "782 gear," which consisted of all the many pieces of equipment, until we knew where each piece belonged and how to produce it upon demand. No superintendent of inventory could give a more thorough or accurate account of the items for which he was responsible than the successful Marine recruit.

Ask any present or former Marine how they feel about the Corps' pervasive indoctrination in neatness and, with few exceptions, they will tell you that nothing that happened to them before or since has contributed more to the quality of their personal and professional lives or the pride and satisfaction they have achieved in all of their endeavors. If I could prescribe but one course of instruction for all students in all schools, it would be one inculcating the fundamentals of neatness in every facet of human existence.

Perhaps the analogy is crude, but no single trait of human conduct can have more impact in preventing the "dingleberries" of life than neatness.

PUNCTUALITY

"Better late than never."

Not many of us have been spared the cutting sarcasm of that observation by a parent, spouse, boss, friend, or co-worker when we failed to show up on time for an appointment or assignment. We probably also have spouted it first in self-defense when responding to the withering glare of someone we have held up by our tardiness.

Well, the Marines turn that around in a hurry in boot camp. Their version is an unequivocal "Better never than late."

I got the point from the DI's boot applied quite forcefully to the seat of my pants the first time I was the last member of my platoon to finish a meal and fall in formation.

We recruits were allotted fifteen minutes to eat, clean and stack our stainless steel serving trays, and then fall in formation again outside the mess hall. The application of the instructor's boot was the undeviating penalty given three times a day for the individual bringing up the rear.

Under the revised and refined rules of treatment followed by today's Marine Corps, kicks and four-letter epithets by DIs no longer are sanctioned, but even the current euphemisms and implied threats are sufficient to give traumatic tremors to trainees who fail the strict standard of promptness. Our entire platoon received a lecture in purple prose about the consequences to combat units when members do not perform their assignments precisely on time. It was made graphically clear in language that always will be remembered that punctuality in military units can, and often is, a matter of life or death.

The lecture goes like this:

> "Suppose two Marine combat patrols are assigned to meet at a certain place and one Marine causes one of the patrols to be late. While waiting, the patrol on time is seen by the enemy who opens fire on it. At the least, buddies would be wounded or killed, and, at worst, an entire battle could be lost."

The old adage about "for want of a nail, a horseshoe was lost; for want of a horseshoe, a horse was lost; for want of a horse, a battle was lost" is quoted with considerable hyperbolic license. And to make certain the point is not lost upon the Southerners in the platoon, it is explained how the Battle of Gettysburg may have been quite different had the revered General Robert E. Lee not been late on the first day.

This all may sound harsh, but there is a purpose to it. In the first place, Drill Instructors have a limited amount of time to teach, and the recruits have an equally limited amount of time to learn it. The lesson of punctuality could be the one that saves the lives of all the members of the platoon at one time or another.

Broadcast journalists Jim Lehrer and Bernard Shaw, both former Marines, have each attributed the discipline of time learned in the Corps as a major factor in their success as respected daily newscasters. And Don Imus, the tough and talented New York talk show host and another former Marine, will raise hell with an interviewee who calls in 20 seconds late. To which I say, "Go get 'em, Don."

Punctuality is a lesson that I learned well and follow religiously in all of my daily schedules, often to the complaints of my fellow workers that I am a "control freak" and place too much emphasis upon the clock.

But I do not think I place too much importance on it. In fact, I believe that being late and keeping someone waiting is about the rudest thing one person can do to another. It says to others that "My time is more important than your time, and I regard myself as being more important than you."

I believe with all my heart that one simply cannot show respect for others if one does not respect the time of others. When several people or a group are kept waiting, the insult and disrespect are multiplied by as many people as are kept waiting for you.

I liked it when report cards sent home to parents by the schools indicated the number of times students were tardy. Teachers who overlook tardiness pay the price of having undisciplined classrooms, and the same is true for principals who do not place appropriate emphasis upon punctuality in their schools. No winning athletic coach ever tolerates tardiness on the part of his players, since domination of the clock is often the decisive factor in athletic competitions.

Tardiness is a disease. It is a disease which feeds upon itself, and I believe that chronic tardiness is symptomatic of even more serious emotional or personality flaws.

The importance of the demands, as well as the constraints, of time in Marine Corps training cannot be overemphasized. Keeping recruits "scared to death" or at least "apprehensive of the consequences" is a learning device that indelibly imprints habits which serve recruits well throughout their lifetimes.

First impressions are important, and it simply is impossible to make a favorable first impression if one is late. The Chinese say that a picture is worth a thousand words, and I believe that being ten minutes late for a job interview says far more than that about you. Tardiness is an insult to the person kept waiting, and I can guarantee anyone who doubts it that being late for a job interview will cost the applicant the job every time.

One cannot be on top of a situation if he or she is late. One cannot control the action in any given circumstance if others have to start without you. At best, one cannot know what has transpired before his or her arrival, and, at worst, someone else can and probably will make decisions for you.

I always have followed the rule to put myself in the other person's shoes when I am scheduled to have a meeting. That attitude has served me well.

When Russia had a czar, no one had a watch and no one could tell time. After the Bolshevik Revolution, Lenin and Stalin had people shot for being late. Emphasis upon time and punctuality was part of the Communist pattern for changing everything in the Soviet Union. (Lucky for us and the world, they did not learn as much about some of the other basic values cited in this book).

It is true there was a lot of rough treatment in boot camp, but one must keep in mind that it was a process designed to produce a man who had respect for himself and others and who could perform effectively in combat.

Ever since boot camp, I have believed that life itself is much like combat. Life is a struggle to wrest success from the odds favoring failure and to achieve the satisfaction of overcoming the spiritual and physical challenges that confront the individual striving to be all that he can be, striving to make the world a better place for his loved ones of today and his descendants of tomorrow.

The Marines teach recruits that the fittest are the ones who survive, and the lessons one learns — like punctuality — will be crucial to survival.

BROTHERHOOD

Outside observers simply "don't get it" when they try to portray the unique character of Marine Corps cohesion and unity of purpose and action as fraternal. It is much more than mere togetherness or collegiate camaraderie. It is brotherhood in its purest form, a bonding of disparate individuals into a common relationship which transcends race and color, religion and beliefs, ethnic origin and cultural background, and places of residence.

Truly, the Marine Corps has succeeded in achieving what democratic society has sought, but failed so far, to attain — the subordination of individual wants and desires to the attainment of the highest aspirations and ultimate goals of the group as a whole. In short, in the Corps the common good is placed first and foremost in all efforts, and attention to individual welfare and goals is always secondary.

I am a living, breathing example of how the Corps refocuses the vision of the individual to the big picture of life and his place and mission in it.

I was a "hillbilly" in the broadest sense of that derisive

term. I came out of the Appalachian Mountains of North Georgia, an area of the purest Anglo-Saxon stock that can be found. And I had a harsh mountain twang to match. The Marine Corps mixed me with young men of all types and classes — first-generation sons of immigrant parents who talked about growing up in "Sout Chicargo," products of the poverty of the Hamtramck part of Detroit, the disdainful youngsters of "The Big Apple" who never let anyone forget they were from "Noo Yawk," blacks from the ghettos and white boys from Alabama, Georgia, and Mississippi who still were fighting the Civil War just like they learned from their "granddaddies," Texans with double first names, and Midwesterners who trusted everyone and New Englanders who trusted no one. We also had a few Hispanics and even two Native Americans, who were called "Indians" then.

Our platoon was a microcosm of the entire United States of America, a little domestic melting pot housed in one crowded quonset hut. We were all in it together, and it did not take us long to get over our mutual suspicions of each other and realize that we all were going to sink or swim, perish or survive together. If we had any doubts of that fact, the DI dispelled them with his little welcoming speech.

"You people are whaleshit," he bellowed, "and whaleshit is the lowest thing on earth; it's on the bottom of the ocean. If any *one* of you screws up, *all* of you will pay the same price for that *one* man's failure. When I speak, you will function as a team. You are all in this together as a team. Do you understand that?"

At that particular time in 1953, not a one of us probably had any notion of who Dr. Martin Luther King, Jr., was. But even if we could not articulate the thought then, we would come to understand during the next twelve weeks what Dr. King meant when he later declared, "We must live together as brothers or perish together as fools."

Nowhere on earth during that three-month period were there 74 more different individuals who learned quickly how to suffer and survive together as brothers — sometimes, admittedly, scared-to-death brothers. Platoon 311 was our world, and we became painfully aware that we would either endure its rigors collectively or be booted out of its ranks individually.

Four decades have passed and the military services are now the most integrated part of America. In present-day society in this country, race is more polarized than it ever has been; and the military services are the best example we have where men and women are getting along and achieving side-by-side regardless of skin color, racial origin, or cultural or religious background.

As one who has seen firsthand how integration works in the Marine Corps, I cannot help posing the question for myself and all citizens: "Shouldn't that tell us something about the correctness of the way the military deals with the problem and the obviously wrong way that society-in-general is going about coping with it?"

It saddens me very much to realize that, within the short course of my adulthood from duty as a Marine to service as the governor of a state, we have met ourselves coming back on the subject of race relations. Mistrust between the races has real consequences. In modern America, blacks are more likely than whites to be victims of crime. Poll after poll shows black voters favor tougher law enforcement measures — from stiffer sentences to the death penalty — in greater numbers than whites. Black-on-black crime is an epidemic in many of America's cities. Yet many black political leaders refuse to support tougher law enforcement, even though it would help more blacks than whites. Why? Mistrust between the races.

There are far more whites than blacks on welfare. And both groups hate the system, which is a universally acknowledged disaster, trapping whole communities into generations of dependency, sapping the vitality and destroying the hopes of the very people it was designed to help. Yet many black political leaders oppose real welfare reform — even though it would affect more whites than blacks. Why? Mistrust between the races.

And some white liberals make the whole situation worse by buying into the argument that things like tougher law enforcement and welfare reform are really punitive measures aimed at blacks. These people are wrong. Black folks have the same right as whites to the dignity of a job. So why do some white liberals oppose tougher law enforcement and welfare reform? Again, mistrust and misunderstanding between the races. I sometimes think they are, in effect, saying, "We expect less from blacks than we do from whites."

To which I can only respond, "What kind of brotherhood is that?"

It certainly is not the kind of brotherhood I learned in the Marine Corps and which I have tried to practice in my personal and public lives ever since. Coming from where I did and enduring the ridicule heaped upon the four of us Marine recruits who were hillbillies from the Ozarks and Appalachia, it was not lost upon me what Merle Haggard meant when he sang about living with the fact that "another class of people put us somewhere just below."

In Platoon 311, the rule was "equal opportunity for all, special privilege for none." The DIs were truly color-blind, equal opportunity persecutors to whom each of their human charges was just another flesh-and-blood mechanism awaiting the tender mercies of their hands-on instructional techniques. They did not discriminate in the giving of rewards, nor did they discriminate with the administration of punishment as they taught their lesson of all men being equal.

That important lesson followed me into civilian life and public service and caused me to feel the wrath of bigots and to be called a "nigger-lover" more times than I care to recall. And, ironically and inexplicably, I have lived long enough now to experience the criticism of liberals for holding the same views for which I used to be excoriated by conservatives.

There were five of us who left Macon, Georgia, on a hot August morning in 1953 for Parris Island — four older and bigger white guys and one young black lad from Atlanta who did not weigh more than 120 pounds dripping wet. We laughed at him behind his back and asked ourselves, "This is a Marine?" But it was not lost upon us that he ended up as one of the leaders of our platoon and was selected to carry the platoon guidon when we marched. He later became a star on the boxing team of the Second Marine Division; and those of us who earlier had derided him subsequently boasted of our friendship with him.

The brotherhood we learned through example and association was translated into teamwork as a unit. We turned into a living, breathing machine as we performed the weekly cleaning of our barracks, which was known as "field day." We donned our blue bathing suits and worked shoulder-to-shoulder in three teams — one swabbing the floor with hot soapy water, the second scrubbing every square inch with brushes, and the third wiping up every drop of the soap and water with squeegees. It was no accident that the floor, or "deck" as we were required under pain of dire punishment to call it, was turned into a gleaming, spotless slab of concrete through our efforts.

Through teamwork we learned how to respond as one to orders and carry them out in concert and to accept the strict discipline under which we learned anew how to do everything from eating to sleeping, from dressing to bathing the right way. Our individuality was sublimated, and, in its stead, we were transformed into a hard working unit. We learned how to accept discipline, and, above all, we learned that we could depend upon our fellow Marines and that they could depend upon us.

When we graduated from boot camp, we left for our new assignments in full confidence that we could perform, together with our fellow Marines, any task which subsequently might be assigned to us; that we could always depend upon the Corps; and that the Corps could depend upon us to support and defend our nation, our freedom, our fellowman and our loved ones.

All of which causes one to wonder, Why can't such a spirit of brotherhood and teamwork be inspired to motivate and energize all of us, individually and collectively, to make our nation and our society all it can be for all of us, regardless of race, color, religion, or status?

PERSISTENCE

Persistence is an instinct with which all babies are born. It is the life force which teaches them to cry until someone picks them up to feed or comfort them. It is the inner nature which causes them to get up when they fall and try again until they learn to walk. It is the motivation by which we learn to ride a bicycle, catch a ball, and play a musical instrument.

That is why the first story read to four-year-old youngsters enrolled in Georgia's pre-kindergarten program is *The Little Engine That Could*, which teaches the most important lesson that I believe can be learned: perseverance. We give children this book to take home and keep and have it read over and over by their parents. It's a good lesson for the parents as well. By the way, Georgia is the only one of the fifty states that makes pre-kindergarten available to all four-year-olds whose parents want it.

Abraham Lincoln never served as a United States Marine, but he typified the strongest of the traits I define in this book. Lincoln has been my example for staying the course since I first heard from my mother the story of his learning to do arithmetic sums using a charred stick on the back of a shovel before the light of an open fireplace on the dirt floor of his log cabin home. There is also a lesson in the number of times Lincoln was defeated for public office: five out of eight attempts.

What would our history be if he had not had persistence and just given up after some of those stinging defeats? I, too, have felt the sting and humiliation of defeat at the polls. And I have had that daunting experience enough times to know how it can numb a man to the depths of his soul. There is only one good reason why I ever made it to be governor of Georgia, the tenth largest of the United States and the site of the 1996 Centennial Olympic Games. It is the same good reason that made Abraham Lincoln the sixteenth, and probably the greatest, president of the United States. It is persistence! Perseverance!

I did not get to be governor because I am the smartest person in my state — far from it.

I was not elected because I have a striking appearance — to the contrary, "average" is the most generous adjective that could be applied to my countenance.

I do not come from a large population center, my home place being a mountain village of 200 located on the remote northern boundary of the state.

My voice would never qualify me to deliver the six o'clock news on television, being a harsh mountain drawl characterized by one reporter as "barbed wire."

My family did not and does not have any wealth, and I was brought up the son of a single mother who had to scratch out a living the best way she could after my father died when I was an infant.

I lost two congressional races before I turned 40 and a senate race before I was 50. I was told over and over in no uncertain terms by people who thought they knew it all that I could not make it in big-time politics and I might as well give up.

I not only was defeated badly in those first two races, but I was left without a job and practically bankrupt, so destitute that to put groceries on the table I had to sell the small personal library that I had so painstakingly accumulated. My wife, Shirley, and I had to take out a second mortgage on our house, which took us years to repay.

But I never forgot a story I had once heard. I do not know whether it was actually true or apocryphal, but I know it stuck with me and inspired me in times of defeat and when my spirits were so low that the only adjective that could describe them was *subterranean*.

It was about a high school senior who applied to three colleges only to be rejected by all three. Finally, when a fourth rejected him, he wrote to the admissions office something like the following:

"Dear Admissions Officer: I am in receipt of your rejection and, quite frankly, sir, that is over my limit, so I am rejecting your rejection and will report for college on September 18th."

I do not know whether that ploy worked for that young man or not, but I liked his attitude and adopted it and made it work for me. It was the attitude that worked for Abraham Lincoln; and it worked for one of his illustrious successors, Theodore Roosevelt. Teddy Roosevelt was rejected when he tried to join the Army after the Spanish-American War broke out. They told him he was too old and, besides, he was too nearsighted. But he rejected the rejection, went out and organized a civilian militia which he christened "The Rough Riders." He packed eleven pairs of glasses into his saddlebags, went to Cuba, and led his followers in their famous charge up San Juan Hill. The rest is history.

A graduate student named Albert Einstein had his doctoral dissertation rejected by the University of Bern as "too fanciful and irrelevant." Fortunately, he rejected the rejection and did not throw his theory of relativity into the nearest wastebasket.

John Grisham, the acclaimed author of such best-selling novels as *Runaway Jury, The Firm, The Client, The Pelican Brief, The Chamber,* and others, had his first novel, *A Time to Kill,* rejected more than a dozen times before a publisher took a chance on printing a few thousand copies. Think how many great books and outstanding movies we would have missed had he not rejected his many rejections.

As I stated earlier, my reason for joining the Marines was to get myself straightened out; but once I was in the Corps, I decided I wanted more than anything else to earn the Expert Marksman Badge like my cousin, Eric England, who was a career Marine and a member for many years of the Marine Corps Rifle Team. He later was a sniper in Vietnam, and his skill with both a rifle and a pistol were legendary throughout the Corps and our mountain area. I knew I never could hope to shoot like him, but I did want — like I never wanted anything before — to belong to the elite group of less than ten percent of all Marines who had the honor of wearing that impressive, and coveted, badge.

Before we recruits ever were permitted even to go near the rifle range, we had to learn our rifles better than we knew our own anatomy. The alternative as our DIs assured us, was that their rifles would become part of our anatomy. We drilled with our rifles, and we slept with them. We learned how to tear them down, clean them, and reassemble them by repeating the process hundreds of times.

The first days on the range were devoted to everything except firing the weapon. We learned the different shooting positions — prone, sitting, kneeling, and off-hand (standing); how to sight; how to let out one's breath properly; and how to "squeeze it off," hopefully into the black bulls-eye. We spent hours, to use the Corps' terminology, "snapping in," that is, getting into absolutely correct positions, aiming the rifles, and simulating shooting time and again at that little black dot on a white post which, at times, seemed a hundred miles away.

Then, during shooting week, we arrived each day on the

range at daybreak in a long firing line with another group waiting behind us to take our places. We moved from the off-hand to the sitting and kneeling positions and then back to the 500-yard line for the prone position. We did rapid fire and slow fire while similar groups of Marines were assigned to what was called the "butts," pulling the targets up and down and marking and scoring each shot.

As hard as I tried, I managed only to make "Marksman." That was "qualifying," but it meant I would leave boot camp without realizing the goal for which I had diligently (and, believe it or not, prayerfully) striven. I swore then I would not give up, and, since all Marines have to renew their qualification with the M1 at regular intervals, I kept working on it even after I was assigned to Camp Lejeune, North Carolina. My buddies thought I was crazy for "snapping in" after the work day, but they did not have Eric for a cousin and did not want that badge as much as I did.

I finally won it just barely with a score of 220 out of a possible 250, and later I even had the thrill of being assigned to coach other Marines on the range for awhile. I loved it. It was the best duty I had while in the Corps. All the sweat, aching muscles, breathing exercises, study of windage, and psyching of my mental and spiritual processes were prices which paid off in my earning the badge which no Marine, before or since, ever wore with greater pride than I.

It was a great lesson on the rewards of persistence. I learned then and there that persistence can overcome anything. My whole life since stands in unrefuted proof of that fundamental fact of human existence.

Persistence is what gets the shoes shined right — Marines spending hours getting just the right gloss on them for inspection.

Persistence is what enables Marines to take their rifles apart and put them back together in perfect working order — blindfolded.

Persistence is what makes drill teams perform in perfect synchronization, honing the ability of its members to toss rifles with fixed bayonets and to catch them without getting a scratch.

Marines believe in rote, in doing things over and over until one gets it right, and, once right, doing it right without exception thereafter.

Persistence paid off for me in politics. It is what gave me the strength to try again after defeats and the stamina to attend countless fund-raisers and receptions without appearing to be tired or weary. It gave me the energy to shake hands enthusiastically and repeatedly at one plant gate after another early in the morning and late at night. It kept me going, constantly crisscrossing the state of Georgia, when other members of the campaign team were dragging.

It made me governor of Georgia — twice!

It is the same trait which drove another former Marine, George Jones, the country music legend, to do the 83 takes it took him to get the recording of his classic country hit, "White Lightning," just like he wanted it.

The Marines have learned how to restore and reinforce persistence as the most vital and fundamental of human values. I fear for the future of democratic society unless we, as a people, learn how to do the same.

PRIDE

Being both a mountaineer and a Marine, I probably have an uncommon — or certainly a very intense — perspective on pride as a vital trait in human success.

In fact, I am convinced that pride has gotten a bad rap from some preachers and extremists of all persuasions. Perhaps it all stems from the fundamentalist viewpoint of our Judeo-Christian religious heritage, which embraces the often-quoted adage found in Proverbs 16:18 of the King James Version of the Bible: "Pride goeth before destruction, and a haughty spirit before a fall."

If one regards that truism in its narrow context of vainglorious egoism and vaunted self-importance, I agree with its conclusion. But to my mind, pride is much, much more than lording personal status or material possessions over those deemed to be less worthy or endowed. I define pride as the feeling of self-worth which finds its source in satisfaction from past accomplishments, motivation in present endeavors, and inspiration springing from future aspirations.

Pride is the quality that builds in individuals and groups solid beliefs of who they are and specific goals of all they can be. Those who cannot or will not find that quality within themselves are doomed to lives which at best are failures and at worst are human disasters.

My mother nurtured pride in me. She taught me that mountaineers not only are proud people but also that I, as one of their offspring, should have that kind of pride in myself as an individual and in the heritage from which I sprang. From her I learned early about my forefathers being among the first white men to push into what was Indian Territory when General Winfield Scott was rounding up the Cherokee Indians for what would become known as the "Trail of Tears."

But I never fully comprehended what true pride was all about and why it was so important in the development of a well-rounded personality until I joined the Marines and went through boot camp.

My education on this subject began on one of my first marches as a recruit. In a ritual all platoons used to go through, the DI takes the platoon around the island and as they pass the statue of "Iron Mike," which is one of the landmarks of the Parris Island base, he stops and gestures proudly, "Take a good look at a *real* Marine."

We quickly learned, thereafter, that the first Marines were organized at Tun's Tavern in Philadelphia in 1775, and they played an important role in the Revolutionary War and in all the others since. In the War of 1812, the Marines did all the dirty work, which allowed Navy Commodore Oliver Hazard Perry to write General William Henry Harrison the famous statement, "We have met the enemy, and they are ours."

The same was true with General Andrew Jackson in the storied Battle of New Orleans, which was fought after that second conflict with Great Britain had already been won. Marines again were called upon to do the bloody fighting that the other services did not want to do.

Their uniforms had high leather collars, giving them their fighting name of "Leathernecks," and their numbers before the Civil War often were less than one thousand. The "Marine Hymn" recounts their exploits, referring proudly to their encounters defeating the Barbary pirates in Libya on "the shores of Tripoli" and defending teenagers at a military academy at the Citadel of Chapultepec, designated as "the halls of Montezuma" during the Mexican War. Like the nation, the Marines divided into Northern and Southern branches during the Civil War. (Yes, there was a Confederate Marine Corps.)

In 1915, Parris Island became the site of the toughest and best known military training in history, and it was Marines trained there who fought some of the most heroic battles during World War I. In the famous battle of Belleau Wood, they earned the admiring appellation of "Teufelhunden," or "Devil Dogs," from the Germans, and it was there that the legendary Gunnery Sergeant Dan Daley encouraged his men to heroic feats of valor by charging out of his fox hole with the cry, "Come on, you sons-of-bitches! Do you want to live forever?"

Even more revered as a Marine hero than Daley was Lewis B. "Chesty" Puller, the most decorated of all Marines and the winner of five Navy Crosses. I have never ceased reminding all who will listen that I served under "Chesty" Puller when he became Commanding General of the Second Marine Division at Camp Lejeune, North Carolina, in 1954-55. I have his photograph in my office at the state capitol in Atlanta, and it gives me renewed pride in my heritage every time I look at that stern countenance. It was he who said, "If you're Marine, you're *all* Marine."

World War II was filled with memorable battles won by Marines — Guadalcanal, Tarawa, Guam, Peleliu, Iwo Jima, and Okinawa to name only a few. And I can assure everyone that they will not find a Marine who is a part of the second-guessing now going on about whether the United States should have dropped its atomic bomb on Hiroshima. What a crock! There would have been one million casualties, a large number of whom would have been Marines in the front lines, had not President Truman had the courage to end the war the way he did when he did.

If there are those who need some visual symbol of what pride means to Marines, they have but to look upon the monument in Washington, D. C., of Marines raising the flag on Iwo Jima, an event enshrined in history by what was unarguably the most famous military photograph ever taken. I have a great reproduction of it behind my desk in the Georgia governor's office.

But some of the finest and proudest moments in Marine Corps history occurred in the now-almost-forgotten Korean War — the Inchon Landing, which most military leaders except General Douglas MacArthur thought was impossible, and the thirteen terrible days of retreat from the frozen Chosen Reservoir, in which Marines not only extricated themselves, their equipment, and their wounded but also the frozen bodies of their dead comrades lashed to the bumpers of their jeeps.

Then, of course, there are the memories indelibly imprinted on the minds of all but the youngest of us of what happened in Vietnam: 57,000 American servicemen, many of them Marines, were killed and now have their names immortalized on the black marble walls of the Vietnam Memorial. Meanwhile, "peaceniks" and draft dodgers caused an indecisive government to indulge in even more vacillation and talk out of both sides of our national mouth.

But Marines never have wavered and have added even greater luster to their pride in themselves and their nation in Grenada, the Gulf War, Somalia, and all the other trouble spots which have commanded their attention in more recent years.

General MacArthur was Army through and through, from the time of his birth as the son of an Army general on the American frontier until his farewell at West Point. But as a man of truth and great insight, he would have to acknowledge that a great measure of his success in the South Pacific and Korea was due to Marines.

I often use the expression, "By the grace of God and a few Marines," a catch phrase all Marines like to use when a mission has been accomplished. Its origin can be attributed at least indirectly to General MacArthur. When he made his triumphant "I have returned" landing in the Philippines, he was confronted by a sign put up by the U. S. Marines that read, "By the grace of God and a few Marines, MacArthur returned to the Philippines."

Now, that is the kind of pride I am talking about as vital to human success.

That is the kind of pride I feel every time I hear the stirring "Marine Hymn" and every November 10th when we Marines celebrate the Corps' birthday, and I recall again, as if it were yesterday, the emotional thrill as my platoon double-timed to chow and chanted as we ran, "Lift your head and hold it high, Platoon 311 is passing by. Lift your head and hold it high, the pride of the Corps is passing by."

No one ever will be able to appreciate the difference true pride makes in an individual's life as much as the graduating recruit departing Parris Island as a bona fide Marine. His life will never be the same. He has mastered the discipline of close-order drill and put on muscle in the right places. His head is screwed on right, and he has discovered that he can accomplish anything to which he sets his mind and perform any task for which he has the will.

He has acquired self-discipline, self-confidence, and self-respect, and he will always have a culture of higher expectations.

He has pride in himself, in what he has already done and what he will be called upon later to do, in his mission as a Marine and in his duty to his Corps and his nation.

A Marine knows that pride is the bedrock upon which he will lay the foundation of his life, and on that foundation he will build the structure by which the worth of his existence and the measure of his accomplishments will be judged.

RESPECT

"Hooray for me and to hell with you."

As harsh as that may sound, that is the only way I can describe the pervading philosophy of life which seems to motivate some of our younger citizens. Too many in our post-Cold War society display a total lack of respect for anything and everything — self, peers, elders, superiors, society, government, law, and values — asking only "What's in it for me?"

We see this attitude manifested every day in many ways — lack of respect for one's country, institutions, and flag; lack of respect for one's parents and teachers; lack of respect for laws, be they speed limits or tax obligations; lack of respect for God and His Commandments; and in a number of other ways that allow one to feel good for the moment or to gain an unearned advantage over others.

If any one lesson drummed into the minds and hearts of recruits in Marine Corps boot camp could be characterized as paramount, it is that of demonstrating proper respect in every facet of human existence.

The lesson begins with respect for authority which, in the case of the recruit, is the Drill Instructor whose every word and inflection is to be heeded and acted upon, regardless of how the individual may feel about its wisdom or appropriateness.

It extends to the flag of our country — the symbol of freedom and opportunity for which millions have given their lives. The flag is not merely a piece of cloth to be used as clothing or desecrated by burning. It is the embodiment of the thousands of names on the Vietnam Wall and the personification of my father who fought in World War I and the many friends of mine who were killed in Korea.

I believe just as strongly that citizens should always stand at attention, place their right hands over their hearts, and thank God for that flag and the nation for which it stands, just as I believe they should bow their heads, close their eyes, and join in the appropriate way for all prayers to Almighty God.

The only word which comes to my mind when I view so-called art displays which desecrate the flag, when I see flags burned in any kind of demonstrations, when I encounter flags or parts of flags being used as articles of clothing, and when I witness citizens failing to come to attention, remove their hats, or stand when the flag passes by is *enraged*.

I do a mental "burn" when I witness the flag being raised slowly, as I have witnessed uniformed bands and color guards do hundreds of times. The flag is supposed to be raised rapidly so that it is waving in the breeze at the top of the flagpole while the National Anthem is being played. Conversely, it should be lowered slowly at sunset, and, unless properly lighted, it is not to be flown under any circumstances before the sun rises or after it sets.

And, speaking of the National Anthem, it, too, must be shown proper respect when played. It is disgraceful enough when spectators in the stands at athletic events slouch, talk, and stuff their faces with hot dogs while the "Star Spangled Banner" is performed, but it is outrageous that the athletes on the field — the idols of our children and the spenders of the millions of our nation's dollars paid them for their sporting skills — do the same or worse. Disrespectors like basketball star Chris Jackson who refuse even to stand on such occasions deserve to be booted out of the country which gave them the opportunity to rise from poverty to get college educations and make millions of American dollars.

To my mind, there can be no 50-50 Americans — only 100 percent Americans.

My favorite source of appropriate quotes, Theodore Roosevelt, had one that is apropos to this subject. In a speech to troops at Camp Union in 1917, he declared, "The man who has not raised himself to be a soldier, and the woman who has not raised her boy to be a soldier, neither of them has the right or is entitled to the citizenship of the Republic."

Harsh, yes, but it pinpoints the bedrock truth — no one with insufficient respect for his country and no one unwilling to fight for its preservation is worthy of being a citizen.

I believe with General and Congressman Carl Schurz who declared before Congress in 1872, "Our country, right or wrong. When right, to be kept right; when wrong, to be put right."

It makes my blood boil when posturing journalists like Mike Wallace and Peter Jennings (who has received just about all the honors this nation can bestow, even though he is not a citizen of it) declare that they respect their position as journalists more than their obligation to the United States. Once in a panel discussion, they were asked, if they were allowed to go with an enemy unit and then that unit ambushed American soldiers in combat would they try to stop them or just "roll tape"? Would they not have a "higher calling" to intervene? Both replied they would *not* have a higher duty; they were "reporters," they answered condescendingly.

I found that response incredulous and, most certainly, unforgivable. In fact, I regard what they said to be as traitorous as I do the actions of Minister Louis Farrakhan in going to Iraq and Libya to court the favor of their anti-American dictators.

How can religious leaders and journalists expect to be respected themselves when they refuse to respect the country which made them what they are?

No less important than respect for one's country is respect for one's parents. Authority begins in the home, and we all can see the dire consequences in our society of the erosion of family ties as the cement which holds our society together and makes its values meaningful and its institutions work.

I take seriously the Fifth Commandment and its promise: "Honor thy father and thy mother: that thy days may be long upon the land which the Lord thy God giveth thee."

Death robbed me of my father when I was only an infant, but I never failed to feel his presence because my mother kept his image and values alive and fresh in the minds of my sister and me throughout our years of growing up under the inspiration of his memory.

There are no more basic or vital aspects of our national life than those of family, family ties, and values. Our nation departs from this bedrock fundamental of American life at the peril of its future. I shudder to think of the consequences the United States will reap in the twenty-first century if we Americans do not honor and sustain our heritage of supporting and maintaining the family of husband, wife, and children as the cornerstone of our national unity and the keystone of our national greatness.

I don't agree with Dan Quayle on all issues, but he was right about what the example of television programs like "Murphy Brown" is doing to the fabric of our national life. Of all the threats to our continued existence as a great nation, none is more frightening or eminent than the assault upon family life, the epidemic proportions of illegitimacy, and the glorification of out-of-wedlock child bearing by rock and movie stars who would not recognize a fundamental value of life if it bit them on the rear.

Equally detrimental to our future is failure to respect family and failure to respect the religious beliefs of others.

In boot camp, no one ever so much as vaguely suggested that one's religious beliefs should be altered or influenced to even the slightest degree. Only on Sunday mornings was worship ever a subject of discussion and then only to the extent that all recruits were urged to worship in their own ways and to respect the differences in those ways among us. In all of my twelve weeks at Parris Island, I never once heard the first joking or critical remarks about any Marine's religion, and we had recruits of all faiths present in our platoon.

My mother brought me up in the Methodist Church, and I was taught that Sunday mornings were the time for Sunday School and the preaching service which followed. And, while I still adhere to the doctrines espoused by the Wesleys, I have always felt at home in all the churches and synagogues I have had the privilege to attend during the course of my public life.

Likewise, respect for the deceased and proper funeral etiquette are important, especially in showing admiration and gratitude to those who, like police officers and firemen, give their lives in the performance of their public duty.

One thing I learned from the Marines was how to honor the dead, and I think it tremendously important that all citizens take the time to pay their "last respects" not only to loved ones but also to those who have served us and not let mere impersonal flowers, notes, or cards take the place of our personal presence and expressions of tribute and grief.

Respect for others and their rights is needed more on our highways. Cutting in and out of traffic without regard to the safety of self and others and "shooting a bird" to drivers who offend us are foremost examples of disrespect. We must restore courtesy and the Golden Rule to our driving habits.

Respect also must be restored to the public classroom where, today, more teachers are leaving their honored calling for failure to be supported in their attempts to maintain discipline than because of the inadequacy of their compensation. Students who abuse and threaten teachers need to be dealt with in the same manner the Marine Corps deals with slackers, misconduct, and lapses in decorum and etiquette in boot camp. The Marines put them in "motivational platoons." In Georgia we place these troublemakers in "alternative schools" where they are disciplined and given special attention.

We also must restore respect in our treatment of nurses, doctors, policemen, firemen, and servicemen to assure that those callings continue to attract the services of the best and brightest of our citizens.

And we must put a stop to graffiti and littering as two of the most flagrant acts of disrespect to ourselves as a society. I propose that graffiti "artists" be apprehended and required to clean up their handiwork with toothbrushes and cleanser and that litterers be arrested and sentenced to "police" a mile of sidewalks, gutters, or highway rights-of-way.

Nowhere today is lack of respect more flagrantly flaunted than on the athletic field. The showboating of athletes who do their silly dances and obscene wiggles after scoring touchdowns or making decisive plays on the gridiron is, to my mind, the epitome of poor sportsmanship and an insult to teammates and fans alike. The same is true of those baseball grandstanders who posture gloatingly at home plate after hitting home runs.

These are arrogant displays which offend me and, I believe, the majority of those who pay big bucks to attend today's professional athletic contests and who expect, in return, to witness athletic prowess and not egotistical, self-congratulatory, I-love-me demonstrations. The saddest aspect of all of this is the wrong example it sets for impressionable youngsters who are led to believe that "showing off" is the proper way to behave when one excels in competition.

I like what Texas Coach Darrell Royal once said to a showoff who had done a dance after scoring a touchdown: "Son, next time you get in the end zone, act like you've been there before."

I liked the old, pre-television style when the scorers of touchdowns quietly laid the ball down in the end zone and went back to the huddle; or the classy way in which Mickey Mantle used to jog around the bases after a home run with his head down and eyes on the ground, saying he "didn't want to show up the pitchers."

That was class. That was respect.

Another pet peeve I have about the erosion of respect in present-day society is the rowdy way many parents behave at today's graduation exercises, high school as well as college. I see more such boorish behavior every time I make a commencement speech, and it is reaching the point where graduation no longer is a solemn occasion commanding respect and admiration for academic achievement and prompting heartfelt and dignified best wishes for the promise of futures ahead. The lessons which elders are thus passing on to blossoming generations are not good ones at all and cheapen the high value we all should place on education and the vital role it must play in our future as individuals and a society.

Consistent respect for ourselves and others will go a long way toward solving many of the problems of society.

SHAME

Shame was ordained by God himself as a basic motivation in human existence when Adam and Eve ruined Paradise for themselves by eating the fruit of the tree of knowledge — the proverbial "apple." Whether one accepts this as an allegory or, as most of us Methodists do, God's truth, the lesson for mankind is the same — the more one learns, the more responsibility one must accept for dealing with the consequences of one's actions. To choose wrong over right and to be caught, whether by apprehension or by the condemnation of one's own conscience, must cause one to feel shame, or embarrassment, if you prefer. Failure to be motivated by that shame or embarrassment to straighten oneself out, to make amends or accept punishment where indicated, and to learn not to repeat the mistakes of the past in the future can only compound the consequences.

Oh, I can hear it now — the psycho-babble of those over-educated, well-meaning professionals whose reality quotient soars about 20,000 feet above *terra firma* as they analyze and condemn my "Neanderthal" views on the subject of shame. They will insist that I do not know what I am talking about and that my experiences as a child and a Marine have warped my personality and distorted my views of life. Good-intentioned people will say that I want to bruise the tender egos of children and to thwart the efforts of experts trying to rehabilitate offenders by talking to them about how society has let them down, instead of teaching them that bad things happen to people who do bad things, and that the way to avoid having bad things happen to them is not to do bad things.

Rehabilitation, I have learned from working in all areas of the criminal justice system — probation, corrections, and parole — must come from within the individuals who have engaged in conduct detrimental to themselves and society. It cannot be forced upon offenders from the outside, no matter how clever or articulate may be the psychologist or the behavioral scientist attempting to do so. Until the offender sees his actions for what they are and feels shame for having done them, he is destined to repeat them and to suffer society's penalties for them over and over. That is what recidivism is all about, and all the talk and counseling in the world will not motivate criminals to change their ways until they are sorry and ashamed for what they have done and resolve within their own minds and hearts not to repeat their offenses.

Many times during the course of my public service I have been the target of permissive sociologists who argue that using shame or embarrassment as a disciplinary tool does more harm than good. I heard about it when I ordered the photographs of deadbeat fathers displayed on wanted posters, but it worked. Georgia is now one of the leading states in the nation in the collection of child-support payments from absent, but responsible, fathers. I also heard their moaning when I was successful in getting a law enacted to have the photographs of three-time DUI offenders published in their local community newspapers. But that, too, has worked.

The point I made in the first chapter of this book about there no longer being a stigma attached to illegitimate births is borne out by the fact that out-of-wedlock parenting has reached epidemic proportions. Young men and women alike no longer feel any shame in producing offspring in environments unsanctioned by matrimony. That attitude seemingly is shared by many of the parents of the unwed mothers; that is, at least it was until the State of Georgia began requiring single mothers to live with their children's maternal grandparents and other states began following suit.

What the objectors to using shame to promote desired standards of public conduct fail to either understand or admit is that humiliation is a powerful motivational force. It was not the whipping at school, but the humiliation of receiving it, that once prompted good and acceptable conduct in public schools.

The Marine Corps learned a long time ago that shame can produce positive results in behavior modification that no other degree of threat or form of force can achieve. The most graphic example I can give is in teaching recruits the correct and precise nomenclature for all their gear, especially their rifle.

What happened to the recruit who slipped up and referred to his "rifle" as his "gun" not only indelibly imprinted the error on his own memory but also served as an enduring lesson to all of the comrades in his platoon who were forced to witness his humiliation.

The errant Marine was forced to march naked up and down the row of racks with his M1 rifle in his right hand and his crotch in his left, shouting over and over, "This is my rifle . . ." as he raised his rifle high over his head, "and this is my gun . . ." as he squeezed his crotch.

Neither that recruit nor any of his fellow recruits ever made that mistake again.

Let me give a couple more examples.

In my platoon, on the afternoon of the first day, a recruit raised his hand and asked permission to go to the restroom. The DI laughed derisively and responded, "Can't you hold it? Then pee in your pants, you little girl." Rendered speechless with embarrassment, the recruit was then ordered, "Go ahead and squat down like a girl while you're doing it." When he hesitated, the DI thundered, "Do it!" And the recruit, red-faced with embarrassment, squatted and visibly wet his pants as he relieved himself.

This prompted a wave of giggles followed by an eruption of laughter on the part of the entire platoon, which brought the following shouted tirade from the DI: "Do you think it's funny? Well, why don't all of you take a leak. Go ahead, girls, squat down and make a sound like you're peeing. You better not pee, but you better make the sound."

Not a one of those humiliated young males ever will forget the embarrassing picture of our squatting on the hot pavement and hissing. Not a one of us ever again even so much as snickered at a fellow recruit's embarrassment.

Shame stings. And the sting stays with the individual so stung. I submit such stings are a powerful means of shaping behavior.

Art Buchwald likes to tell of his experience after laughing at a recruit in another platoon who was being disciplined. The DI made the recruit put a bucket over his head and yell over and over, "I'm a shit bird." As punishment for laughing, Buchwald was required to put a bucket over his head, stand at attention in public for a long time, chanting over and over, "I'm a shit bird, too."

"Bleeding hearts" probably will call such treatment "dehumanizing," but its purpose is to produce men who will be effective in combat, and the record of the Marine Corps in doing that for 200 years is proof positive that it works. In fact, history records that military discipline has worked for thousands of years in bringing order to otherwise unorderly lives of men who have been called upon to defend their native lands, their homes, and their families.

Being singled out for unworthiness, ineptitude, ignorance, or slovenliness worked wonders in shaping up recruits to perform with precision in close-order drill or to qualify as experts and sharpshooters with the M1 rifle. Those who seemed unable to master the technique of marching in cadence were deemed unworthy to be a part of the platoon and were not allowed to march with it. Those who had difficulty distinguishing between their left and right feet had the offending foot promptly stomped by the drill instructor so a throbbing left foot became a constant reminder to "do it right."

The worst thing that could happen to the Marine who experienced continued difficulty in getting into the shooting positions demanded by the Primary Marksmanship Instructors was to be assigned to the "eight-ball squad" for additional instruction. After a week of intensified indoctrination in that outfit, which included hours of "snapping in" and correctly getting in and out of the positions, the Marine was either pronounced ready to resume regular training or he was gone for good. Although some always flunked out, the majority chose "shaping up" over "shipping out."

The Marine Corps brand of shame made many determined men out of bewildered or wayward boys. There never has been a better or more proven way to get and keep an individual's attention than the profane and crude, but unforgettable, Marine Corps way.

Nobody wants to go through life being known by the lowest of Marine Corps characterizations. There is nothing that can focus a "foul-up's" resolve to get his "act in order and his ass in gear" more clearly than a red-faced DI shouting into his face, "Boy, you're lower than the nipples of a snake!" Or, "Were you sent here to make my life miserable?"

I want to see a society in which inspiration to succeed and determination to avoid the humiliation of failure are equal incentives in inspiring all children to grow up to be all that they can be.

RESPONSIBILITY

"Take what you want, sayeth the Lord, take it and pay for it."

I was a grown man before I learned that quote was not from the Bible; it was just my mother's holy script. But I also came to the concurrent realization that, even if it were not part of the Holy Writ, it should be, because I do not know of any more fundamental truth that can be imparted from deity to subject or, in my case, from mother to child.

That truth has been a guiding principle of my life, especially since I got my head screwed on straight in Marine Corps boot camp. To me it means individuals can have anything they want out of life if they are willing to work hard enough to earn it. One can be a star basketball player, if one practices hard enough, and one can make good grades in school, if one studies long and hard enough. Perhaps the greatest single flaw in the fabric of today's society is that too few seem to understand or accept that basic concept for living successful, meaningful, and contributing lives.

Many people today seem to want everything given to them. Children do not want to lead disciplined lives. Students do not want to study. Few people, it seems, want to work, especially not if the task is hard and the hours are long.

Everybody wants dessert, but few are willing to eat spinach to get it.

The fruits of labor come only to those who first labor for the fruits. That, perhaps, is a truism, but my mother believed it, and she and my boot camp Drill Instructor ultimately made a believer out of me.

Responsibility, personal and collective, is one of the first lessons taught to Marine Corps recruits, and it is so thoroughly drummed into the minds, hearts, and souls of those who make it through boot camp that it becomes as much a part of their existence as a second name or a tattoo across the chest.

A Marine learns that in the Corps he is responsible not only for himself, but also for all of his fellow Marines. (In the case of boot camp, those who are members of his platoon.)

He is responsible for all of his gear, down to the exact number of tie-ties, which he must keep immaculate and be able to lay out in a precise manner on his rack for periodic inspection at any given time.

He is responsible for his appearance under penalty of severe punishment for a stray whisker or a disorderly crease.

He is responsible for his rifle, which must be sufficiently clean at all times to stand white-glove and Q-tip inspection without turning up even so much as a single speck of dust or spot of oil.

He, and all of his platoon mates, are responsible for the

cleanliness of their barracks, its head, and the surrounding grounds of the battalion; and everyone is turned out to correct any deficiencies in any of those venues whenever discovered.

An integral part of the lessons we were taught on responsi-, bility was that Marines really are their "brother's keepers," just like God impressed upon Cain after he had slain Abel. And the DIs make their point about Marines being responsible for each other by imposing group punishment for the offenses and mistakes of individual recruits. In other words, when one recruit messes up, the entire platoon is disciplined.

It was a source of great pride to me that no one in my platoon ever had to pay the price for my "goofing off" or "fouling up." It was not lost upon me that those who did cause such pain for their comrades usually suffered a second consequence that night after lights were out. One would not be surprised at how quickly this can focus the attention of a recruit who has caused his platoon to drill an extra hour because he was out of step.

My mother and wife were puzzled by my practice of disciplining my two sons in the same way. My sons once had a Little League baseball coach who could not understand why I wouldn't allow either of my boys to play in an important game because one of them had gotten into a fight the day before. But I did not have any further problem with either fighting.

I believe that fathers should be held responsible for the children they sire and that mothers should be responsible for the children they birth. Nothing has done more to bring us to the sad and low point society has reached in the state of family values than this failure on the part of parents of both sexes. That is why I have been in the forefront of those advocating laws to put the photographs of "Deadbeat Dads" on wanted posters and to revoke the business, professional, and drivers' licenses of those who flagrantly refuse to support their children as well as laws to require teen-aged mothers to live with their parents and complete their educations and adult, single mothers to take job training and go to work.

But this is a two-headed coin, because I believe just as strongly that children must be responsible for the parents who cared for them when they were helpless after the parents become infirm and are unable to look after themselves.

My mother was a strong woman until her health failed in her eighties. We hired people to provide for her until it became an around-the-clock proposition; after which we heeded the firm advice of our family physician to put her in a nursing home. It was the hardest decision we ever made.

Her once lean and almost muscular body deteriorated and her creative mind and quick tongue produced only gibberish. I remember how it became necessary for me to clean her after a bowel movement, but I did it willingly and gladly while reminding myself, "She once did the same for me. This is my responsibility now."

Fathers have a responsibility to support their children, but the mother's responsibility is even more basic. Since most of the brain cells of a body develop in the first few months the fetus is in the womb, the mother who does not have proper nourishment is likely to produce a baby with fewer brain cells, and the mother who drinks alcohol or uses drugs may have a baby that is severely damaged, perhaps retarded.

I take pride that Georgia is setting a national example with its highly successful Workfirst Program to get adult mothers off welfare rolls and onto payrolls without penalizing them or their children. We feel that it constitutes "welfare reform without meanness." No one ever said that reforming welfare would be easy, but everyone with any degree of human compassion knows that the mean-minded approach of simply taking bread out of the mouths of babies is not the way to go. Our approach is to give mothers the proper instruction and encouragement *and* to assure that their children will not be denied day care and medical services while their mothers get on their working feet. These mothers will get out and learn how to support themselves and their families, and their children will grow up to have normal lives as individuals who can hold up their heads with dignity and personal pride.

Parents also must be inspired, or, if necessary, required, to provide guidance, example, and discipline through the teen years of their children. These aspects of growing up cannot be left to chance any more than can the provision of nourishing and balanced diets.

I believe that parents should be held responsible for the acts of their teen-aged offspring. Crimes by 13-year-old juveniles were virtually unheard of when I was growing up, and now we are faced with an epidemic of murders, rapes, robberies, and other adult crimes by children not out of middle schools. Parents more and more are giving into peer pressures exerted by the wildest and least responsible of those in their childrens' age groups. The wailing cry of the teenager denied permission to do as he or she wants is, "But Johnny or Suzy is doing it!"

Children need not only to be told what they can and cannot do, but they also must see examples set by their parents. Everyone with any common sense knows that children do not do what they are told; they do as their parents do. Fathers and mothers can preach until their tongues fall out about the evils of alcohol, but children who witness their parents drinking are going to imbibe, too. You can count on it. Bigoted fathers can expect to have bigoted children, and scofflaws can expect their offspring to have no respect for either laws or policemen enforcing them.

There are family and economic circumstances which force children to be latchkey kids left at home to their own devices when school is not in session. While not a desirable or recommended situation, this arrangement can work if responsible parents define and emulate responsibility before their children and demand the same from them.

I believe a major factor in current trends of lawlessness among youths is no-fault divorce, which has made it all too easy for both men and women to shirk their parental responsibilities. Once marriage produces children, it should be made exceedingly difficult for the parents to divorce. When I was growing up, adults unhappy in marriage compromised and stayed together "for the sake of the children." We need more of such selflessness on the part of parents who seem today to give top priority to their own happiness and comfort rather than thinking about the welfare and future of their child or children.

Responsibility is what life is all about, and it should not be as easy to shirk or discard as last year's fashions.

And that goes for journalists, both print and electronic, too. I believe in freedom of the press as much as the next fellow. In fact, I have been the editor of a newspaper during the course of my checkered career. But I do not believe that editors or reporters have any right to create news or to interpret happenings anywhere except on the editorial pages.

Television particularly has become the principal educator of today's society, and it has a responsibility which far transcends showing pictures of blood and gore and titillation of prurient appetites with no redeeming values, designed solely for increased ratings.

Responsibility to me means conducting oneself in a fashion that, if one's conduct does not contribute to the betterment of society, as least it does not denigrate its goals or depreciate its values in any way.

ACHIEVEMENT

As one who has survived to senior citizenship, who has reached and passed the "over-the-hill" landmark of 65 birthdays, and who has been there, done that, and seen it all all around the world, I can attest of my own observation, experience, and knowledge that there are only two kinds of people on this planet: There are talkers, who constitute the overwhelming majority; and there are the doers, who, for good or bad, constitute the minority.

I have a friend who insists there are really *three* kinds of people — the few who make things happen; the greater few who watch the lesser few who make things happen and then criticize; and the vast multitudes who do not know anything is happening until it already has happened and often not even then.

While I stick to my thesis of there being only two kinds of people, I will concede that my friend makes a valid and supportable point.

In my field of government, I observe the differences between those who talk about it and those who do it.

Some of our most able and smartest people fall into a sub-classification of talkers — those who complain and gripe about everything, those who always know a better way to do everything, and those who just talk and talk and talk.

These are people who could make real contributions if only they would stop pondering and start doing. Another friend refers to those who refuse to take active roles in political affairs as suffering from the "Gray Sickness," meaning that many of those who have the "gray matter" will not participate in public affairs.

One of my heroes always has been Theodore Roosevelt, whom I love to quote and who seems to have had a quotable passage on every subject of importance. And, of all his many wise sayings, the one I have liked, believed, and repeated the most is, "The credit belongs to the man [and, I would add, woman] who is actually in the arena, whose face is marred by dust and sweat and blood; who strives valiantly; who errs and comes up short again and again . . . who at best knows in the end the triumph of high achievement; and who, at the worst, if he fails, at least fails while daring greatly. So that his place shall never be with those cold and timid souls who know neither victory nor defeat."

Teddy Roosevelt would have made a great Marine — one we Marines would call a "gung ho" Marine, which means one who is highly motivated and hard working; the Chinese term translates as "work together."

And I am certain that Teddy, were he alive and still making his memorable speeches today, would say to the talkers what he said to his Rough Riders when they were training for duty in Cuba up on the banks of the Tennessee River west of Nashville: "I want to see you shoot the way you shout."

The one thing DIs despise the most and tolerate the least among recruits at boot camp is idleness. The schedule they enforce without exception is one in which every minute, except the six to eight hours per day spent sleeping, is programmed for some type of work. One of the first things the DI states upon the arrival of recruits is, "I never want to see you doing nothing. You have shoes to shine, a rifle to clean, and a guide book to study."

Bull sessions were as *verboten* as was daydreaming. Boot camp lights were extinguished exactly at 2100 (9 p.m.) and reveille was between 0300 and 0500 (3 and 5 a.m.), depending upon the next day's schedule. Sack time was much too precious to be wasted either in conversation with others or solo contemplation.

The recruit never knew at what time during the day he and his comrades might be called to attention to spout their knowledge on the "30-caliber M1, air-cooled, gas-operated, clip-fed, semi-automatic shoulder weapon," or to recite such things as General Orders or "My Rifle," a long recitation, part of which went as follows:

"This is my rifle. There are many like it, but this one is mine. My rifle is my best friend. It is my life. I must master it as I must master my life. My rifle without me is useless. Without my rifle I am useless. I must shoot straighter than my enemy who is trying to kill me. I must shoot before he shoots me. I will. . . . My rifle is human, even as I, because it is my life. . . . I will keep my rifle clean and ready, even as I am clean and ready. . . ."

No recruit ever was able to fault any DI for not working harder and longer than anyone else in the platoon or failing to set the proper example at all times. DIs have the most demanding job in the Corps and work up to 110 hours a week during the early weeks of boot camp — an example in the work ethic which is not lost upon the recruits.

Each platoon had its schedule of M&M (Mess and Maintenance) duty where every recruit spent one week as a cook's helper in the mess hall. This meant a 17-hour work day spent either in a steaming kitchen or a freezing cooler. Rise-and-shine time for M&M duty was 0300, even earlier than for training, and the nonstop assignments that followed made every recruit appreciate his chow even more and stifle any complaints he might have about it.

If there were a mantra at Parris Island, it was "You are not a Marine. You are a recruit. You have to earn the right to be a Marine." That was repeated to recruits over and over during their training.

In many respects my DI reminded me of my mother, who was the hardest worker I had ever known before I encountered him. She never sat down on the front porch to rest or gossip with the other women in Young Harris, Georgia, who were often heard to say about their lazy husbands, "He doesn't work hard enough to break the Sabbath."

I was further reminded of my boot camp indoctrination in the work ethic when I first met A. L. Williams, who went from being a high school football coach to a multi-millionaire insurance executive. In his great self-help book, Williams tells the story of someone watching Masters' champion Gary Player hit a golf ball and gushing, "I'd give anything if I could hit a golf ball like you."

The great South African golfer, according to Williams, gave the questioner a withering stare and replied, "No, you wouldn't. You know what it takes to hit a golf ball like I do? You get up early and you hit a thousand golf balls. Your hands begin to bleed and you rinse them off with cold water and then you hit a thousand more. That's what it takes to hit a golf ball like I do."

The renowned British writer, Rudyard Kipling, put it this way in his *Epitaphs of the War:* "Body and spirit I surrendered whole to harsh instructors — and received a soul."

I often have reflected upon what great benefit all of the human race could derive from running a "confidence course" like Marine recruits are required to do in boot camp. I think it would be a great revelation to those who do not realize what they could accomplish if only they took the action needed to achieve their goals and realize their potential.

Many businesses have realized this and, accordingly, send their top executives to participate in the "Outward Bound" Program in which they go through obstacle-course-type challenges to build their confidence and to inspire them to greater heights of effort and achievement in their business leadership.

The confidence course is one of the last big hurdles recruits have to overcome to graduate from boot camp. It consists of a dozen obstacles through which each recruit must make his way within the allotted time; each obstacle is more difficult and demanding than the one before. It is a daunting challenge to both the body and spirit of the recruit, and even the most physically fit among the trainees are rendered pale and trembling by the sight and thought of what they are being called upon to do. At a very minimum, one must be fast and agile and not afraid of heights. My first reaction to the prospect of surviving was typical: I trembled in my boots and said to myself, "I'll never be able to do that."

The obstacles range from scaling an eight-foot wall sloped toward the runner to swinging on a rope across a pond of water said "in jest" to be populated by alligators to climbing a cargo net like the one Marines use at sea to debark onto landing craft. Then one takes the skin off his hands sliding down a rope, climbing another cargo net to the height of a three-story building, and then descending hand-over-hand upside down while holding on to the rope with both hands and crossed legs over another pool of water in what was appropriately called the "Slide for Life."

After having done this successfully for the required three times, the recruit has his confidence so pumped up that he is convinced he can do anything. This kind of training is exceptionally hard, but it is remarkably successful in teaching a person not only the ultimate of his or her capability but also his or her capacity for enduring physical challenges and mental and spiritual stress.

No Marine, once he has successfully completed boot camp, ever again will doubt his or her ability to perform any and all assigned tasks or to carry out demanding assignments to the satisfaction of themselves or their superiors.

COURAGE

I never would be so presumptuous as to claim that I am courageous or that I ever have done or said anything that required any great demonstration of courage on my part. Only time, circumstances, and the judgment of history can make such a determination.

But I do know courage when I see it, and I know that Marine Corps training has turned out many heroes whose courageous acts have been incontrovertible and inspiring.

Two of them are Georgians and are among the half dozen congressional Medal of Honor winners I have had the honor to know during my lifetime: Major General James E. Livingston, Jr., who won his highest decoration for valor in the rice paddies of Vietnam, and General Raymond Davis, who was one of the greatest heroes to come out of the frozen hills of Korea.

Both are mild-mannered and unassuming, but I challenge anyone to talk with them for even the briefest period of time without being impressed by their steely demeanor, which says more eloquently than their citations that they are truly special.

There are different kinds and varying degrees of courage. These two exceptional Americans proved they have the ultimate of that attribute in battle, and both have told me they were able to accomplish their feats because of the lessons they learned as Marines.

They agree with that anonymous sage who once observed, "The difference between a coward and a hero is one step — sideways," and they share the conclusion that the Marines teaches all who wear its symbol not to take that step.

They also concur with Ralph Waldo Emerson, who said, "A hero is no braver than the ordinary man, but he is braver five minutes longer." And they agree that the Corps has mastered the secret of instilling the will and inspiring the determination in Marines to hang in there those extra five minutes.

Mark Twain could have been talking about Marines when he said, "Courage is resistance of fear, mastering of fear, not absence of fear." Everyone has fears, and there are few among us who have not experienced absolute terror at one time or another during our lives. But it is those who can take physical stands against threats or make mental or spiritual resolutions not to be swayed in their convictions that prove themselves stronger than their fears.

There are many ways that courage can be displayed. Courage is what makes the difference between a statesman, who does or says what he truly believes is right before such thoughts and actions are popular, and a politician, who says what he thinks people want to hear and leads the crowd only after he observes the direction in which it is going.

John F. Kennedy wrote a Pulitzer Prize-winning book, *Profiles in Courage*, about political courage. He observed that "to govern is to choose," and I can attest that I have had to make such choices from time to time during the course of my public life, and I can but hope that I have demonstrated a little of that kind of courage in some of the difficult choices I have had to make.

I have referred several times in this book to my mother and the courage she demonstrated to my sister and me in hauling the rocks out of the cold mountain stream to build our house and in working harder and longer than anyone I ever have observed to eke out a living for her children.

But those are not the kinds of courage I want to address in this chapter. Instead, I want to cite the examples of two personal friends — one, my mentor among Marines, and the other, my idol among the many athletes I have known and followed since I first picked up a baseball bat in Young Harris, Georgia, and fantasized myself to be the reincarnation of Babe Ruth and Lou Gehrig rolled into one.

The first is Master Sergeant George Burlage under whom I served in the Marines and who still lives, and the other was the legendary (to my mind, the greatest in history) baseball player, Mickey Mantle, who recently succumbed to failure of a liver transplant.

Mickey, the baseball Hall of Famer, spent much of his last five years of life in Georgia, living on a golf course he dearly loved on Lake Oconee about an hour west of Atlanta.

I got to know him well. We visited often, and we hit it off from the beginning — he the star of the diamond and I just another baseball wannabe. We were two small-town boys who each made it to the "bigs" in his own way, he much more significantly in the national pastime of baseball in the world's largest media center, New York City, and I in the statewide politics of Georgia as governor.

I went out to see Mickey after his transplant operation in a hospital in Dallas. I learned upon my arrival in the Texas city that his body was rejecting the transplant, and the prognosis for his survival was not good. When one of his sons, Danny, came to pick me up the next morning, I suggested that perhaps I should not make the visit, but Danny insisted, saying that his Dad wanted to see and talk with me.

We arrived at the hospital to find a television truck parked outside with its antenna up, and when we entered through the back way and went up to the fifteenth floor, we found his room guarded by a policemen who had been stationed there to keep away the milling reporters and, especially, the vultures of *The National Enquirer*.

I asked Danny to go in first and make certain everything was all right, and when he motioned for me to enter, I encountered Mickey standing nude bathing himself with a soapy washcloth just as he had done hundreds of times before in crowded locker rooms where modesty is not an imperative.

His hair was wet and down on his forehead. A huge incision stretched across his stomach from one side to the other and then up his chest for another six to eight inches. The incision was stapled in neat surgical precision, and there were shunts in his chest and neck for the injection of medication.

As Danny rummaged through a brown paper bag for some white pajama bottoms, Mickey gestured to his legs and said in mock derision, "Look at these wheels! They're pitiful! They're like a girl's!" (And it was hard to believe that those legs once had carried an 18-year-old Oklahoma boy faster from home plate to first base than anyone who ever had played the game.) His once-massive right arm was swollen and had turned dark purple from his shoulder down to his forearm.

Mickey carefully combed his hair, applied some deodorant to his armpits, pulled on a T-shirt, and then staggered trying to put on some socks. I thought he was going to fall and could not help momentarily replaying in my mind's eye that classic clubhouse scene in the movie, "Pride of the Yankees," in which Gary Cooper playing Lou Gehrig did fall while pulling off his socks.

"You need some help," Danny said, rushing over to put his Daddy's socks on for him.

We made small talk while he dressed, and I found that, even in his physical pain and mental torment, he wanted to play one of the practical jokes for which he was renowned. He put on a rubber mask (which Danny had brought him) of an old, wrinkled man with a ragged fringe of white hair framing the ears. He said it was for my benefit when I told folks back in Georgia how he was doing.

We talked some more, and I learned how terribly upset he was about the stories some reporters were writing about his getting a liver ahead of someone else. He also talked wistfully about the possibility of perhaps getting another transplant.

His other son, David, came in, and I rose to leave, not wanting to stay too long. I hugged him gently and told him I would see him back in Georgia.

"I hope so," he said softly and sadly.

Those were his last words to me, and two weeks later I was back in Dallas to attend his funeral.

During the interval, this remarkably gifted athlete and great, all-around human being gave the world an unforgettable example of how to die with class and courage.

I always will cherish my memories of him and never will cease to try to live up to his example.

I purposely chose to withhold my account of George Burlage, the man I always will know with great affection and unbridled admiration as "Top," because my life experience with him pre- and postdated that with Mickey. Ironically, "Top" still lives near Dallas, where Mickey died.

Now nearly 80, Burlage is as rough and tough as ever, reinforcing my belief that "Top" was indestructible and would continue in life as long as the Corps itself.

He told me of his desire to visit Andersonville, Georgia, and to see for himself the infamous Civil War Prisoner of War site where a POW Museum is being built. I told him I would be overjoyed to make the arrangements and invited him to come to Georgia as my guest and to stay at the Governor's Mansion while he was there. Colonel Ben Purcell, another former POW, and I accompanied him to Andersonville.

To Master Sergeant George Burlage, the prisoner of war experience was more than the graphic pages of some book — it was a personal experience which he had endured and miraculously survived during World War II.

"Top" had been out of Japanese prisons less than 10 years and had served another demanding tour of duty in Korea when I served under him.

He had been captured on Corregidor early in the war and spent three years in various Japanese prisoner of war camps in the Philippines and in Japan. He saw most of his comrades die, and he was subjected to beatings, torturous work details, and periods of starvation when no food was given to him for days. Since most POW experiences are too horrendous for those of us who have not gone through them to understand, I know he was inclined to understate them, but, based on what I learned from his accounts, I always will hold in total awe and utmost admiration those who lived through such hellish ordeals.

"Top" suffered from malaria, acute dysentery, beriberi, and pellagra and saw his weight drop from 200 to 108 pounds. But he endured it for three years and even lived through being stacked like cordwood with other prisoners in the hold of a ship and transported to Japan. He and the others had no food or water for four or five days, and twenty to fifty men died each day, the weaker being so demented from thirst that they would try to bite open the throats of others for a drink of blood. The living lay side-by-side with the dead until the bodies were hauled out and dumped overboard.

Few lived through that hell, and those who did so survived only because they had courage beyond belief.

Of all my heroes of all times, George Burlage is at the top of the list. Whenever I feel discouraged, disheartened, or weary, I make it a point to think of "Top" and all that he suffered and overcame, and I always feel renewed in body and spirit.

No human attribute is more needed, or more sadly lacking, in today's climate of expediency and self-gratification than courage, and I thank God nightly that the Marine Corps is one agency of society that continues to inspire and instill it in present and coming generations.

DISCIPLINE

One normally would not think of the lowly, pesky sand flea as an effective teacher of one of life's most basic lessons for success — the absolute necessity for discipline.

But any Marine Corps recruit who has survived the rigors of 12 weeks at Parris Island can attest to the fact that that hellish pest was an integral element of the cram course in wisdom otherwise known as boot camp.

There must have been at least a million of those seemingly-ubiquitous bugs assigned to my platoon, and I would have sworn that the overwhelming majority of them picked me out to be teacher's pet.

I entered boot camp the last week in August when "hot" would have been much too mild an adjective to describe the heat. Even "scorching" seemed inadequate to delineate the penetrating temperatures which turned trainees into sopping sponges within a couple of hours of marching.

But that was the least of the discomforts and irritations which accompanied the summer climate of the South Carolina low country. Sand fleas were everywhere, and gnats were flying escort and urging their "cousins" on. They got in our eyes and crawled into our ears. Every breath sucked one or more of them into panting mouths or exploding nostrils. And everywhere one found a landing spot, it commenced to bite, which felt as if it would suck all of the blood out of you.

Each one was an irritant that would not go away. The only relief the victim could imagine was to slap and, hopefully, kill the attacker. But that was only temporary, at best, because there were always two more to take the casualty's place.

That would have been bad enough, but the DIs compounded the agony by constantly yelling into the red faces of the suffering recruits, "Don't slap that sand flea! You had your chow, now let him have his!"

Next to the exclamation, "I can't hear you!" which trainees heard over and over again, this was the one order heard most in boot camp.

Recruits who would, or could, not obey that order — and more often than not swatting was as involuntary as a twitch of the eye — were punished on the spot. A slap at a flea would bring an even harder slap or a kick in the rear from the DI. Killing one would result in an order to bury it.

And I do not mean bury it in a little hole in the ground, but rather to dig a grave which could be up to four feet long, three feet wide, and several feet deep, depending upon the mood and whim of the DI. God forbid that the recruit should find himself unable to produce the corpse which, under the best of circumstances, would be a bloody little speck.

Burial duty for a sand flea produced remarkable results in

terms of renewed tolerance for all the countless relatives that succeeded it. It was a sadistic, cruel, harsh, and even brutal ritual — which would have been hilarious had it not been taken so seriously — but it had its purpose. Like close-order drill and other things done in boot camp, it was designed to instill discipline — not only to obey orders promptly and fully, but even more importantly to develop the resolve and motivation within oneself to do whatever is required to perform one's duty, be it to self, the Corps, or the nation.

An orderly life is built upon discipline, and the Marine Corps is nothing if not disciplined. Discipline is the mortar which holds together all of the other values, like punctuality, that I have enumerated and discussed in this book.

No military unit can exist — let alone fight — without discipline.

Discipline is paramount.

Discipline teaches one that every whim cannot be gratified nor can one indulge in every desire, no matter how compelling. Take the case of the sand flea. If the recruit cannot discipline himself to withstand the irritation of one little insect or to bear the momentary pain of its bite, how can the finished Marine survive and prevail when lying in a swamp with the enemy all around, when one movement well may give away his position and that of his platoon?

So, as any Marine can testify, the sand flea is a mighty teacher.

Discipline with persistence can overcome virtually any

obstacle and resolve nearly any difficulty. That philosophy has stood me in good stead throughout my public career.

Days and nights on the campaign trail have gotten so long and tiring that I have found myself hardly able to go on. Many times I have had to force myself to get up to meet a late-night or early-morning shift change at some plant. Many times I have found myself so weary at a reception or cocktail party that I would go into a restroom and sit on the toilet with my pants up for a few minutes just to get a second wind and pump up my resolve before going back into a crowded room to keep going with the handshaking and socializing so necessary for success in politics.

I have developed a lifelong habit of disciplining myself to practice discipline, and, by that, I mean that almost daily I make myself do something I do not particularly want to do.

Sometimes it is to exercise. Other times it is to turn off television and read a book I need to read. I make it a practice when I am particularly tired to make myself do just one more thing so that my lazy psyche will know that I will not listen or give in to it.

I make myself write even though I do not want to make the effort, and I am certain some of my critics will make the point that this is evident in my writing.

I often will get up earlier than usual (and that is really early) and do something that needs to be done just to show myself I can still do it.

My wife, Shirley, says this is "weird," but I will even loiter around a pastry counter inhaling the delicious aroma of the bakery smells and then not buy any of the goodies, just to prove to myself that I still have the discipline to reject them.

You see, I believe that discipline must constantly be exercised like a muscle, because, like a muscle, it will atrophy and grow weak if it is not used.

To get back to the sand fleas, I fortunately never had to use the discipline I developed at Parris Island not to slap one in a combat situation, at least not in a combat situation with guns. But I can vouch for the fact that, when I have run statewide political races in Georgia and gone south "below the gnat line," discipline has come to my rescue many times, and I can blow away gnats out of the corner of my mouth while orating out of the other with the best of the stump speakers.

City slickers from Atlanta or upstarts from North Georgia are often unnerved and always annoyed during their first political rally and barbecue in deep South Georgia, where it seems the gnats get to do more eating than they. Being from the North Georgia mountains, I would have been in bad shape in situations like that had it not been for my boot camp experience.

I just discipline myself and let the gnats eat away, hearing all the while my DI's voice of many years before ringing in my ears:

"Don't slap that sand flea! You had your chow, now let him have his!"

LOYALTY

Of all the human instincts, the strongest and most basic is the will to survive. An essential ingredient of that will is a well-defined sense of belonging, an identity with one's roots in family and society, and an appreciation of one's heritage in both its broadest and narrowest aspects. One can call this sense many things, but loyalty covers it perhaps as well as any other generic term. The Marine Corps defines it at its succinct best in its motto "*Semper Fidelis* — Always Faithful."

Those two Latin words and their English counterparts are what set the Marine Corps apart from all other military organizations. They are the driving force that has made the Corps the best and most respected fighting force the world has ever known. And they are inseparable in their meaning, both enduring and uncompromising, and constituting an incomparable tie that binds disparate individuals into a united whole.

I have worn a miniature Marine insignia — the famous globe, eagle, and anchor which symbolize the Marine function to fight on land and sea and in the air — in my lapel for many years. Hundreds of times I have had men, and lately women, as they pass me in an airport or we meet at some function, glance at it, and call out, "Semper Fi." And whenever I hear it I know that I have met a fellow Marine or a close associate or relative of a Marine.

There is nothing like it. It is the cement which binds the brotherhood (and I mean that in its nonsexist context) together. It is loyalty — loyalty to the Corps, loyalty to fellow Marines, loyalty to the tradition that is the Corps, and loyalty to the American nation and everything for which it stands. It is the famous *esprit de corps* that sets the proud and the few apart.

In my own case, I was luckier than most. I had the virtue of loyalty pressed deep into my soul long before I'd ever met my drill instructor at Parris Island — by a leader more impressive than the most fearsome Sergeant Major: my mother, Birdie Miller.

She believed — and taught me to believe — that loyalty, like charity and all the virtues, begins at home. At its most elemental, loyalty must be given by children to their parents, to their siblings, to their family. From there, like ripples in a pond, it radiates out to neighbors, to the community, the region, and the nation. But it starts with the family.

People without a sense of family — and without a sense of place radiating from that deep core of family — have no meaning in their lives. They might as well be amoebas existing solely to gobble up everything that comes within their touch and never giving anything back to the environment which nurtures them. Which is why, in a desperate and doomed search for that missing sense of family and place, too many turn to self-destructive behavior like abusing alcohol or other drugs, joining gangs, and breaking laws. In a sick and sad way they are creating their own "family," their own sense of place — a sense of at least belonging to something, even if it's the lowest of the low.

When I see homeless, broken people sleeping on park benches in our greatest cities, or hollow-eyed drifters lined up for free meals at compassionate churches and missions; when I have seen the soulless stares of prisoners who have shattered innocent lives, I think about how tragic it is that their lives are meaningless vacuums of existence, without anything larger than themselves to believe in. Without anything to be loyal to. And with nothing and no one who is loyal to them.

My mother would have been quite a Marine. She knew instinctively that loyalty begins as a one-on-one relationship. And so it sounded oddly familiar when my friend and mentor in the Marines, Master Sergeant George Burlage, told me there was one reason he and his fellow Marines who had been captured by the Japanese during the Second World War survived — loyalty. And not just loyalty to an abstraction, some vague notion of democracy or freedom. More fundamental than that, they survived because they were loyal to each other. They didn't break under pressure, wouldn't crack under torture, couldn't just lie down and die, because they didn't want to let their buddies down.

You ask a Medal of Honor winner, or anyone who has shown great courage under fire, what could possibly override their powerful, primal instinct of self-preservation, and nine times out of ten you'll hear the same answer: "I didn't want to let my buddies down. They were counting on me." In a word, loyalty.

I saw many who came into the Marine Corps without the strong foundation my mother gave me — young men with voids in their lives who found a sense of family, a sense of place, a sense of loyalty, in the Marines. The "Semper Fi" tradition of the Marines has been more than two centuries in the making, and I have never encountered a force as powerful in motivating and maintaining loyalty, or as influential in giving direction to lives. The power of loyalty made those hollow men full. I believe it can do the same for millions of others who feel their lives lack a sense of purpose, of belonging to something greater than themselves.

When I became governor, it was loyalty that kept me from getting a big head and making big mistakes. I always knew where I came from and where I was going back to.

In the North Georgia Mountains, from which I get my sense of place, we have a saying, "If you ever see a turtle on a fence post, you know one thing: it did not get there by itself. Someone put it there." And today, in the governor's office that I walk into every day, there proudly hangs a picture of a turtle on a fence post. It's a constant reminder of the good friends and the folks who put this old turtle up on this high fence post.

I have strived every day, in every way, to meet that simple but powerful goal Master Sergeant Burlage told me was the greatest motivator of all: never let your buddies down. In this case, "buddies" have been replaced by the people of Georgia. And like every Marine — and every civilian with a strong sense of loyalty — I would rather die than let my people down.

As a family member, I cannot forget who put me "there."

And, as one of many Marines, I can attest that we, individually and collectively, never forget who put us "there" — who made us the most elite of the fighting force in our history. I think it safe to say that I speak for all Marines when I state we will always be faithful to those Marines who came before us and to those who come after us.

Loyalty is the thread which holds together the fabric of humanity. It is a timeless virtue. One of the greatest sins of all time was a betrayal of loyalty when Judas betrayed Jesus with a kiss.

But loyalty is also a tricky virtue. It's easy enough to say we should be loyal, that we should not be a Judas. But what do we do when we're faced with conflicting loyalties? When being loyal to one value may call on us to sacrifice another? I believe it is in these gray areas, in the half-light between right and wrong, that strong, clear, core values are needed most.

We all wrestle with moral dilemmas, and politicians as much as the rest of us are torn when loyalties collide. I remember being dumbfounded by what I thought was the disloyalty of my longtime friend, Jimmy Carter, when as President he granted unconditional pardons to the draft dodgers who had fled this country rather than serve in an unpopular war. Like many, I remember thinking the pardon was disloyal to the men who had served and to the veterans and military leaders who felt they had not been adequately consulted.

But in time I have come to realize that this Annapolis graduate, this protégé of the great admiral Hyman Rickover, was trying his best to sort out deeply held, yet divided, loyalties. On the one hand, he owed a debt of loyalty — as a veteran and as Commander in Chief — to those who were then serving and those who had served in the past. But on the other hand he believed he owed a higher loyalty to his Christian principles of reconciliation and forgiveness and to his duty as President to move the country past the bitter division of that terrible war.

Truth is, I might have made a different choice. But in the end, all we can ask of our leaders is that they define and defend their loyalties. There have been times in my own life and career when I have been accused of disloyalty, and nothing hurts me more.

Perhaps the most costly, from a political point of view, was when I chose to devote nearly all my energy to an all-out effort to restore Georgia's state flag to its original design, before segregationists in 1956 added the Confederate battle flag. As the descendant of heroic men who fought and died in the Lost Cause, I owe a deep debt of loyalty to their valor. They bravely risked their all for what they believed in — and they believed in far more than slavery, because some of my ancestors were not exactly of the plantation-dwelling, slave-owning class!

But as governor I owe loyalty to *all* the citizens of my state. And as a historian I owe loyalty to the truth. And the truth is, the Confederate battle flag under which my ancestors fought with honor was shamefully hijacked by segregationists nearly a century after Appomattox. Hatemongers added that symbol to our flag to show contempt for the court rulings that called for an end to segregation. They took a noble symbol and perverted it, using it to intimidate the powerless and divide Georgians.

Some said I was being disloyal to my Southern heritage and my Confederate ancestors. But I don't see it that way. I saw my fight to restore our flag as keeping faith with our true history, restoring the dignity of our past, ending the division of the present, and working toward unity in the future.

Unfortunately, the Georgia Legislature — and the vast majority of Georgians — didn't see it that way. It was the most unpopular thing I have ever done. My effort to restore the original flag and remove the Confederate battle flag was overwhelmingly defeated. Polls showed my popularity plummeted. Yet I was re-elected the next year, anyway, in part, I think, because even those folks who disagreed with me came to believe I was acting in good conscience. Acting from my own sense of loyalty, drawn from those North Georgia mountains, my mother's teachings, and the United States Marine Corps. Once again, I was saved by having strong values and stating them clearly.

EPILOGUE

For want of a better term, it was "core values" which made our nation great as we established and built the most envied and admired country in the shortest period of time in the recorded history of mankind. By "core values" I do not refer to religious dogma or theology to which each of us subscribes according to our individual faiths, but rather to the broad characteristics which constitute the difference between a responsible and contributing human being and an unconscionable savage bent upon taking or destroying whatever they want that they are unable or unwilling to earn for themselves.

The relationship between the erosion of our standards of personal conduct and the deterioration of the moral character of our society cannot be explained away. The fact is that we are the top among nations in rates of divorces, unwed births, and abortions. We lead the industrialized world in murder, rape, and violent crime, to say nothing of the damning statistic that we are at the bottom in achievement scores in elementary and secondary education.

That there are those in positions of influence and authority who seem to have a complete indifference to the downward spiral of human condition is incomprehensible to me. They ignore the fact that our founding fathers had a word for such a human condition and it was *anarchy*. Our brethren, the French, in their quest for freedom and democracy, learned from the excesses of the French Revolution that there can be too much of either. If it is unbridled, freedom can rob mankind of the vital distinctions between humans and the lower animals.

It is appalling for me to hear well-meaning and otherwise brilliant educators contend that values cannot be taught in the public schools, because to attempt to do so would infringe upon our First Amendment right of speech and religion. No one of any intellectual depth would contend that schools should attempt to teach or even influence the spiritual beliefs of individual hearts and souls; that can, and rightly should, come only from the individual homes and churches of each person. The values to which I refer in this book are more fundamental than that. They are the broad-based principles which should govern human behavior, regardless of the tenets of a particular religious faith.

The values of diversity tempered by commonality to the benefit of all are the ones that I had indelibly imprinted upon my psyche in Marine Corps boot camp. I believe with all my heart that they are the same values upon which the survival of America's culture depends. I submit myself as proof that they can be instilled within a given period of time and without the slightest degree of compromise to one's religious beliefs, the theology to which one subscribes, or the deity one worships. Of all the many complaints I have heard about Marine Corps indoctrination, any variations on that theme were not among them.

It will not be easy and it will take time, but somehow we must reconstitute the family as the bedrock unit of society. And by family I mean married fathers and mothers living in homes in which their children are wanted, protected, nurtured, and educated to become productive adults who live contributing lives and who recognize that their world will be no better than the niches they establish for themselves in it.

While I am alarmed by what could happen in society if present trends continue to erode our values, I do believe with William Faulkner, who declared in his acceptance speech for the Nobel Prize in 1950, "I decline to accept the end of man."

Man, said this Southern genius of the pen, alone among the creatures of the earth "has a soul, a spirit capable of compassion, sacrifice and endurance." It is that distinction that I learned at Marine Corps boot camp. It is that distinction which I strongly believe will set those of us who care what happens to civilization back on the road of the pursuit of the basic values of life which I had to learn the hard way in boot camp.

There was a news photograph I recall from the days of college demonstrations against the Vietnam War which made an enduring impression upon my mind, one that I carried with me over the years and remember to this day. It was of a protesting student carrying a sign with the words, "Nothing is worth dying for."

I did not believe that to be a true assessment of most Americans then, nor do I believe it to be accurate now.

Surely, if there is nothing worth dying for in our America, then there is truly nothing worth living for here, either. If I did not believe that before going to Marine Corps boot camp, I most certainly was a believer after I graduated.

It is a truth I want to see indelibly impressed upon the hearts and minds of all young Americans growing up today. It is one which has kept me living, working, striving, and persevering over the years. And I am convinced it is one that will be the salvation of our nation and its coming generations if we will but impart its values to them now.

Now, while there is yet time to save us as individuals and as a nation.